T0039784

Foreword.

This volume is a sequel to our previously published
and now widely used Easy Classics To Moderns and More
Easy Classics To Moderns (Numbers 17 and 27
in the Music for Millions Series). The piano
literature of nearly three centuries is represented
by these original compositions of medium grade difficulty.
All selections are in their original form, neither re-arranged
nor simplified. They are set in approximately chronological order.

CLASSICS TO MODERNS

In The Intermediate Grades
Compiled and Edited by Denes Agay

Marks of phrasing and expression are often editorial additions
especially in the music of the pre-classical period.
These signs were added for a quicker and easier understanding
of the structure and mood of the compositions. They are to be
considered as suggestions rather than rigid directions. Students,
teachers and all pianists should find these original piano
works valuable for study, recital, sight reading or just
inspired musical entertainment of the highest caliber.

The Publisher.

Order No. AM 41617
International Standard Book Number: 0.8256.4037.7
Library Of Congress Catalog Card Number: 62-22540

Music Sales America

DISTRIBUTED BY
HAL•LEONARD®
CORPORATION
7777 W. BLUEMOUND RD. P.O. BOX 13819 MILWAUKEE, WI 53213

Contents

Air

Henry Purcell
(1659-1695)

Saraband

Henry Purcell

Hornpipe

Henry Purcell

March

Henry Purcell

Jigg

Jeremiah Clarke
(1669–1707)

Adagio

from Toccata No. 11

George Muffat
(1645–1704)

Ballet Anglois

Johann Kaspar Ferdinand Fischer
(1650–1746)

Allegro giocoso

* *Play all eighth notes staccato*

Canzoni di Danza

Bernardo Pasquini
(1637–1710)

* *Play all eighth notes staccato*

Fughetta

Domenico Zipoli
(1688-1726)

Allegro energico

Gavotta

Arcangelo Corelli
(1658-1713)

Sonata

Domenico Scarlatti
(1685–1757)

Toccata

Leonardo Leo
(1694-1744)

Capriccio

Domenico Scarlatti
(1685-1757)

Allegro moderato

Aria

Johann Kuhnau
(1660–1722)

La Diane

Francois Couperin
(1668–1733)

La Florentine

Francois Couperin

Allegretto con tenerezza

Original time signature $\frac{12}{16}$

Menuett

From J.S.Bach's "Little Note Book
for Wilhelm Friedemann Bach"

Gottfried Heinrich Stölzel
(1690-1749)

Trio*

Johann Sebastian Bach
(1685-1750)

Andantino espressivo

mp legato

cresc.

mf

crescendo

Repeat Menuett

* *Bach wrote this Trio to follow and be part of the preceding Menuett*

Little Prelude

Johann Sebastian Bach

Invention

Johann Sebastian Bach

Fughetta

Johann Sebastian Bach

Allegretto

Gavotte
from French Suite No. 5

Johann Sebastian Bach

Bourrée I

from French Overture

Johann Sebastian Bach

Bourrée II

from French Overture

Johann Sebastian Bach

Allegro cantabile

Allemande

Georg Friedrich Händel
(1685–1759)

Courante

Georg Friedrich Händel

Passepied

Georg Philipp Telemann
(1681-1767)

Musette

from English Suite No. 2

Johann Sebastian Bach
(1685-1750)

Andantino grazioso

Chaconne
Theme And Six Variations

Georg Friedrich Händel

Var. 4

Var. 5

Var. 6

Gigue

Georg Friedrich Händel

Fantasie

Georg Philipp Telemann
(1681-1767)

La Joyeuse

Jean Philippe Rameau
(1683-1764)

Gigue En Rondeau

Jean-Philippe Rameau
(1683–1764)

Allegro

Wilhelm Friedemann Bach
(1710–1784)

L'Auguste

Carl Philipp Emanuel Bach
(1714–1788)

Fantasia

Carl Philipp Emanuel Bach
(1714–1788)

Alla Polacca

Carl Philipp Emanuel Bach

The Juggler

Johann Philipp Kirnberger
(1721-1783)

Solfeggietto

Carl Philipp Emanuel Bach

Allegro Scherzando

Joseph Haydn
(1732–1809)

Polonaise

Wilhelm Friedemann Bach
(1710 – 1784)

Moderato

German Dance

Joseph Haydn

Allegro con brio

Trio

D. C. al Fine

Minuet

Joseph Haydn

Allegro Giocoso

Joseph Haydn
(1732–1809)

Da Capo
senza replica

Viennese Sonatina No.1

First Movement

Wolfgang Amadeus Mozart
(1756-1791)

Allegro brillante

Minuet and Trio
from Viennese Sonatina No.1

Wolfgang Amadeus Mozart

Allegretto

Menuetto da capo

Waltz

Wolfgang Amadeus Mozart
(K.567, No. 5)

Bagatelle

(Op. 119, No. 11)

Ludwig van Beethoven
(1770–1827)

Andante ma non troppo

Bagatelle

(Op. 119, No. 5)

Ludwig van Beethoven

Six Variations On A Swiss Song

Ludwig van Beethoven

Theme

Var. II

Var. III
Minore

Var. VI

Three Ländler

Franz Schubert
(1797–1828)

Five Ecossaises

Franz Schubert

Three Waltzes

Franz Schubert

About Strange Lands and People

Robert Schumann
(1810 -1856)

Norse Song
Greeting to G*

Robert Schumann

* *Niels W. Gade, friend of Schumann*

Rustic Song

Robert Schumann

Improvisation*

Robert Schumann

* On a theme-fragment by Beethoven (Prison Terzett from "Fidelio")

Scherzo

Johann Nepomuk Hummel
(1787 - 1837)

Allegro con brio

Children's Piece

(Op. 72, No. 1)

Felix Mendelssohn
(1809-1847)

Allegro moderato

Song Without Words

(Op. 19, No. 4)

Felix Mendelssohn

Prelude

(Op. 28, No. 6)

Frédéric Chopin
(1810-1849)

Prelude

(Op. 28, No. 7)

Frédéric Chopin

Prelude

(Op. 28, No. 4)

Frédéric Chopin

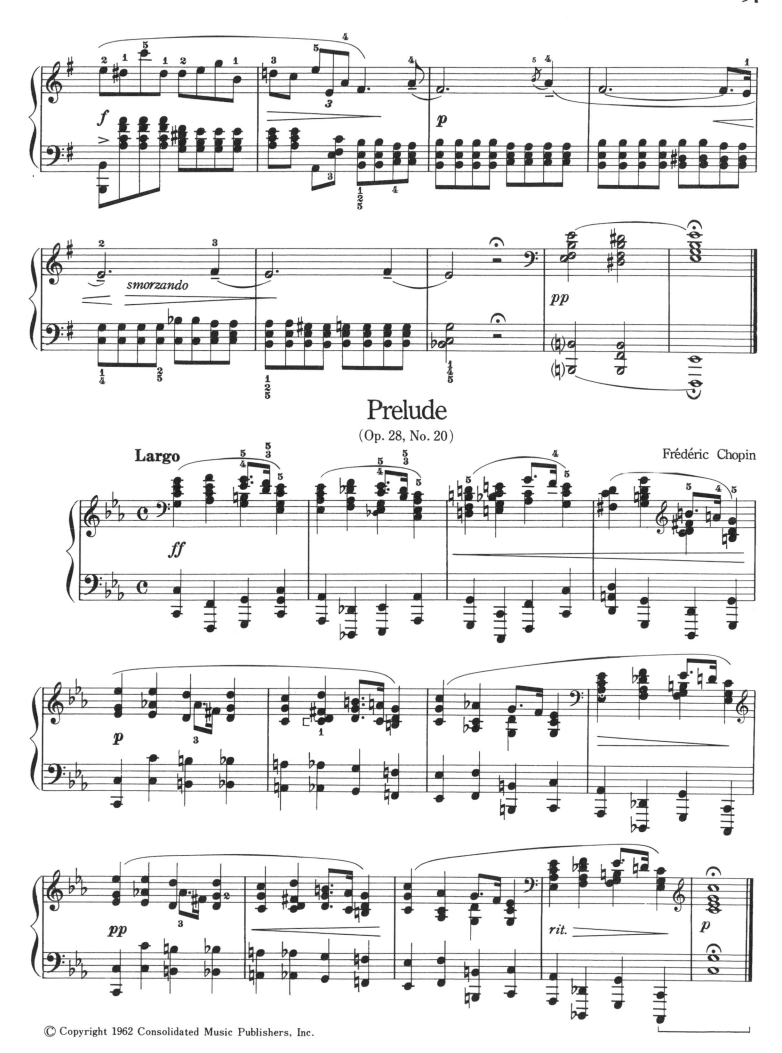

Prelude
(Op. 28, No. 20)

Frédéric Chopin

Mazurka
(Op. 67, No. 2)

Frédéric Chopin,

Tarantella

Michael Glinka
(1804-1857)

Waltz
(Op. 39, No. 9)

Johannes Brahms
(1833-1897)

Album Leaf

César Franck
(1822–1890)

Allegretto delicato

Kamarinskaia
(Russian Folk Tune)

Peter Ilyitch Tchaikovsky
(1840-1893)

Allegro

Polka

Peter Ilyitch Tchaikovsky

Waltz

Peter Ilyitch Tchaikovsky

Intermezzo

Theodor Kirchner
(1823-1903)

The Cowherd's Song

(from Op. 17)

Edvard Grieg
(1843-1907)

Song Of The North

(Saebygga)

(from Op. 17)

Edvard Grieg

Elfin Dance

Edvard Grieg

From A Story Book

Robert Volkmann
(1815-1883)

Allegro giocos

Valses Poeticos

Enrique Granados
(1867–1916)

Allegro humoristico

2

To A Wild Rose
from " Woodland Sketches "

Edward MacDowell
(1861-1908)

Sea Piece

("A merry song, a chorus brave...")

Edward MacDowell

Lively, in changing moods

Frolic

(Op. 17, No. 12)

Max Reger
(1873-1916)

Allegro vivace

Dance With A Bell

Vladimir Rebikoff
(1866-1920)

Kukla
The Russian Doll

Vladimir Rebikoff

Prelude No.4
(Op. 11, No. 4)

Alexander Scriabine
(1872-1915)

Chanson Sans Paroles
(Op. 40, No. 2)

Jan Sibelius
(1865 – 1957)

Andantino

Romance

Reinhold Glière
(1875-1956)

Gymnopedie No. 3

Erik Satie
(1866 – 1925)

Brisk Game

Dmitri Kabalevsky
(1904-)

Allegro assai e marcato

Novelette

Dmitri Kabalevsky

The Horseman

Dmitri Kabalevsky

Allegro molto

Prelude

Dmitri Shostakovich
(1906-　)

Parade Of The Grasshoppers

Serge Prokofieff
(1891-1953)

poco meno mosso

Tempo I

dim. poco rit.

p

cresc.

p

mf

f

Two Brazilian Children's Songs
from "Guia Prático"

1. Farmers' Daughters

Heitor Villa-Lobos
(1881-1959)

2. Goodness!

Fun At Home
from "The Adventures of Ivan"

Aram Khatchaturian
(1903-)

Allegro moderato

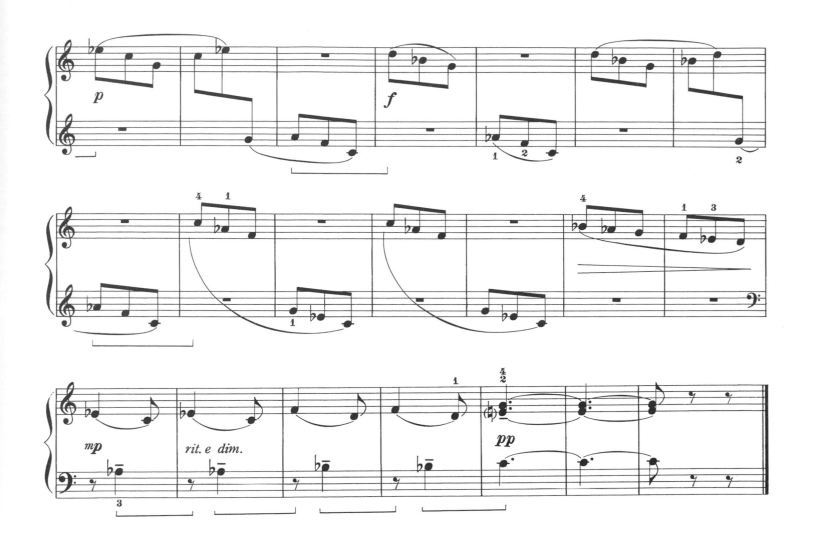

Ivan Is Ill
from "The Adventures of Ivan"

Aram Khatchaturian

On The Playground

Nikolai Rakov
(1908-   )

Allegro con brio

Lament

Zoltán Kodály
(1882-)

Four Hungarian Folk Tunes
1. Courting Song

Béla Bartók
(1881-1945)

Allegro non troppo

2. Play Tune

3. Stars, Shine Brightly

4. Drinking Song

Dawn

Béla Bartók